HOW TO SAFEGUARD YOUR PRIVACY FROM A HIDDEN CAMERA

EXPERT TIPS AND TECHNIQUES TO PROTECT YOURSELF FROM CREEPS, CAMERA, AND UNWANTED INTRUSIONS

MICHAEL S. THOMPSON

Copyright ©Michael s. Thompson, 2024. All rights reserved.

No part of this publication may be reproduced, distributed, or transmitted in any form or by any means, including photocopying, recording, or other electronic or mechanical methods, without the publisher's prior consent, except in the case of brief quotations embodied in critical reviews and certain other noncommercial users permitted by copyright law.

TABLE OF CONTENTS

INTRODUCTION **5**

CHAPTER 1: Understanding Peeping Toms and Hidden Cameras **12**
    Types of Hidden Cameras and Their Uses 16

CHAPTER 2: The Creep Factor: Real-Life Stories and Case Studies **20**
    Unveiling Stories of Privacy Violations 21
    Learning from Others' Experiences: What Went Wrong and How to Avoid It 23

CHAPTER 3: Mastering Awareness: How to Stay Vigilant in Any Setting **26**
    Developing a Mindful Mindset: Being Aware of Your Surroundings 27
    Identifying Potential Camera Locations: Tips and Tricks 29

CHAPTER 4: Tools of Defense: Hidden Camera Detection Techniques **32**
    Introduction to Hidden Camera Detectors 33
    Using Technology to Your Advantage: Hidden Camera Detection Apps 35

CHAPTER 5: Home Sweet (Spy-Free) Home: Securing Your Living Space **39**

Checking Your Own Space: Tips for Home Inspections..............40

Safeguarding Against Rental and Airbnb Camera Risks..................42

CHAPTER 6: Beyond the Basics: Advanced Strategies for Privacy Protection............................46

Maintaining Privacy While Traveling......................47

Legal Considerations and Recourse Options......... 49

CHAPTER 7: Empowering Yourself: Building a Personalized Privacy Plan...54

Assessing Your Privacy Needs..............................55

Creating a Customized Privacy Protection Strategy... 57

CHAPTER 8: Community Awareness and Advocacy: Spreading Knowledge and Taking Action................61

Educating Others About Hidden Camera Threats.. 62

Supporting Legislation and Initiatives for Privacy Rights..................63

CHAPTER 9: Staying Safe in the Digital Age: Online Privacy and Security................................68

Understanding Online Surveillance Risks...............69

Implementing Digital Privacy Measures.................71

CHAPTER 10: Future Trends and Emerging Technologies: Anticipating and Addressing New Threats...........................75

    Exploring Future Risks and Challenges...................76
    Adapting Strategies to Stay Ahead of Evolving
    Privacy Concerns..78

Appendix... **82**
    Glossary of Terms...82
    Additional Resources and References.................... 84
    Frequently Asked Questions (FAQs) about Hidden
    Cameras and Privacy Protection............................ 85

CONCLUSION... **89**

INTRODUCTION

In today's interconnected world, the threat of hidden cameras poses a significant challenge to our privacy and security. Gone are the days when the idea of being watched without consent was confined to science fiction or espionage thrillers. With the advancement of technology and the proliferation of miniature surveillance devices, the invasion of privacy has become a disturbingly real concern for individuals worldwide.

Hidden cameras, also known as covert or spy cameras, are designed to discreetly capture video and audio footage, often without the knowledge or consent of those being recorded. These devices come in various forms, ranging from tiny pinhole cameras concealed within everyday objects like alarm clocks, smoke detectors, or even clothing hooks, to more sophisticated devices equipped with wireless capabilities and motion sensors. Their small size and inconspicuous appearance make them particularly insidious, allowing them to be placed in virtually any location without attracting suspicion.

The proliferation of hidden cameras poses a multifaceted threat to privacy. In public spaces such as restrooms, fitting rooms, hotel rooms, and changing areas, individuals may fall victim to voyeurism or unauthorized surveillance, unaware that their most intimate moments are recorded for nefarious purposes. Similarly, in private settings such as homes, rental properties, or vacation accommodations, hidden cameras can be used by unscrupulous individuals to spy on unsuspecting occupants, violating their sense of security and trust.

The rise of online platforms and social media has also facilitated the dissemination of illicitly obtained footage, amplifying the harm caused by hidden camera incidents. Once captured, compromising images or videos can be shared widely, leading to reputational damage, emotional distress, and even physical harm for those depicted. Moreover, the pervasiveness of digital technology has blurred the boundaries between public and private spaces, making it increasingly difficult to escape the watchful gaze of hidden cameras.

Beyond the immediate privacy concerns, the proliferation of hidden cameras also raises broader ethical and societal questions about surveillance, consent, and the balance between security and individual rights. While some argue that surveillance cameras serve a legitimate purpose in deterring crime and enhancing public safety, others contend that the indiscriminate use of hidden cameras represents a grave violation of personal autonomy and civil liberties.

Importance of Safeguarding Your Privacy

In an era of constant connectivity and digital surveillance, safeguarding your privacy has never been more important. Privacy is not merely a matter of personal preference or convenience; it is a fundamental human right enshrined in international law and recognized as essential to individual dignity, autonomy, and freedom. Without adequate privacy protections, individuals are vulnerable to exploitation, manipulation, and intrusion by both state and non-state actors.

Protecting your privacy is about more than just shielding your personal information from prying eyes; it is about preserving your autonomy and control over your own life. In a world where data is increasingly commodified and monetized, maintaining control over your personal data is essential to preventing identity theft, financial fraud, and other forms of exploitation.

Moreover, safeguarding your privacy is crucial for maintaining trust and fostering healthy relationships in both personal and professional contexts. When individuals feel that their privacy is being respected and protected, they are more likely to engage openly and authentically with others, fostering a sense of mutual respect and trust. Conversely, when privacy is violated or disregarded, it can lead to feelings of betrayal, resentment, and alienation, eroding the foundations of trust and intimacy.

In the digital age, protecting your privacy requires vigilance, awareness, and proactive measures to mitigate risks. This includes safeguarding your personal devices with strong passwords and encryption, being mindful of the information you share online, and staying informed about emerging threats and best practices for digital security.

By taking steps to safeguard your privacy, you are not only protecting yourself from potential harm; you are also asserting your fundamental rights and asserting your autonomy in an increasingly surveilled world. In doing so, you contribute to a broader culture of privacy and respect for individual rights, ensuring that future generations can enjoy the same freedoms and protections that we often take for granted.

CHAPTER 1

Understanding Peeping Toms and Hidden Cameras

The term "Peeping Tom" conjures images of a clandestine figure lurking in the shadows, surreptitiously observing others without their consent. While the term may seem antiquated, the behavior it describes remains a pervasive and troubling phenomenon in modern society. Understanding the motivations and methods of Peeping Toms is essential for addressing the threat they pose to privacy and security.

At its core, the behavior of a Peeping Tom is driven by a combination of voyeuristic impulses and a lack of respect for boundaries and consent. Peeping Toms derive gratification from observing others in intimate or compromising situations, often without their knowledge or consent. This voyeuristic behavior can range from relatively innocuous activities such as surreptitiously observing neighbors through windows, to more invasive acts such as installing hidden cameras in private spaces.

The motivations behind peeping behavior are complex and varied, but they often stem from underlying psychological factors such as a desire for power, control, or sexual arousal. For some individuals, peeping may serve as a form of escapism or fantasy fulfillment, allowing them to vicariously experience the thrill of forbidden voyeurism without facing the consequences of their actions. Others may be driven by deeper psychological issues such as compulsive behavior or a lack of empathy for others' privacy rights.

In terms of methods, Peeping Toms employ a variety of tactics to satisfy their voyeuristic urges while avoiding detection. Traditional methods of peeping, such as peering through windows or using binoculars, have been supplemented in recent years by the proliferation of hidden cameras and other surveillance devices. These miniature cameras can be easily concealed within everyday objects such as alarm clocks, smoke detectors, or even clothing hooks, allowing Peeping Toms to covertly capture video and audio footage of their unsuspecting victims.

The advent of digital technology and the internet has further facilitated the spread of peeping behavior, enabling perpetrators to share and distribute illicitly obtained footage online. Social media platforms, online forums, and dark web marketplaces provide fertile ground for the dissemination of voyeuristic content, amplifying the harm caused by peeping incidents and perpetuating a culture of voyeurism and exploitation.

Addressing the threat posed by Peeping Toms requires a multifaceted approach that addresses both the individual and societal factors driving this behavior. From a psychological perspective, interventions aimed at addressing underlying issues such as compulsivity, empathy deficits, or distorted beliefs about privacy and consent can help reduce the likelihood of reoffending. Legal measures such as criminalizing peeping behavior and enhancing penalties for privacy violations can serve as deterrents and provide recourse for victims.

Types of Hidden Cameras and Their Uses

Hidden cameras come in a variety of shapes, sizes, and configurations, each designed to serve a specific purpose and evade detection. Understanding the different types of hidden cameras and their uses is essential for recognizing and mitigating the threat they pose to privacy and security.

One of the most common types of hidden cameras is the pinhole camera, which is characterized by its small size and discreet appearance. These cameras are typically concealed within everyday objects such as alarm clocks, smoke detectors, or picture frames, allowing them to blend seamlessly into their surroundings and avoid detection. Pinhole cameras are often used for covert surveillance in residential, commercial, and public settings, where they can capture video and audio footage without arousing suspicion.

Another type of hidden camera is the body-worn camera, which is designed to be worn on the person's clothing or accessories. Body-worn cameras can take the form of buttons, pens, glasses, or even jewelry, allowing the wearer to capture video and audio footage from a first-person perspective. These cameras are often used by individuals seeking to record interactions with others for personal or professional reasons, but they can also be used for nefarious purposes such as voyeurism or espionage.

In addition to traditional hidden cameras, there are also more sophisticated surveillance devices equipped with wireless capabilities and motion sensors. These cameras can be remotely controlled and accessed via smartphone apps or computer software, allowing perpetrators to monitor live or recorded footage from a distance. Wireless hidden cameras are often used for home security, nanny monitoring, or pet surveillance, but they can also be exploited by Peeping Toms to spy on unsuspecting victims.

Overall, the proliferation of hidden cameras poses a significant threat to privacy and security in both public and private settings. By understanding the motivations and methods of Peeping Toms and familiarizing ourselves with the types of hidden cameras they use, we can better protect ourselves and others from the invasive intrusion of covert surveillance. Vigilance, awareness, and proactive measures are essential for safeguarding our privacy and preserving our fundamental rights in an increasingly surveilled world.

CHAPTER 2

The Creep Factor: Real-Life Stories and Case Studies

Peeping Toms and hidden cameras are not just figments of our imagination or sensationalized plot devices in movies; they are real threats that have affected countless individuals in their everyday lives. By delving into real-life stories and case studies, we can gain a deeper understanding of the impact of privacy violations and glean valuable lessons on how to protect ourselves from similar experiences.

Unveiling Stories of Privacy Violations

One of the most unsettling aspects of privacy violations is their indiscriminate nature; they can happen to anyone, anywhere, at any time. Consider the case of Sarah, a young woman who discovered a hidden camera in her Airbnb rental during a weekend getaway with friends. What was intended to be a relaxing retreat turned into a nightmare when Sarah stumbled upon the camera hidden in the living room clock. The realization that she had been unknowingly filmed in her most private moments left Sarah feeling violated and vulnerable, shattering her sense of trust and security.

Similarly, the case of Michael highlights the insidious nature of voyeurism in public spaces. While browsing in a department store, Michael noticed a man behaving suspiciously near the changing rooms. Upon closer inspection, he realized that the man was attempting to surreptitiously film unsuspecting shoppers as they tried on clothes. Michael's quick thinking and intervention prevented a potential privacy violation, but the incident served as a stark reminder of the ever-present threat of Peeping Toms in public settings.

These real-life stories serve as sobering reminders of the pervasive threat posed by hidden cameras and Peeping Toms. Whether in the privacy of our own homes or the seemingly secure confines of public spaces, we must remain vigilant and proactive in safeguarding our privacy and security.

Learning from Others' Experiences: What Went Wrong and How to Avoid It

In addition to highlighting the prevalence of privacy violations, real-life stories and case studies offer valuable insights into the factors that contribute to these incidents and how they can be prevented. By examining the experiences of others, we can identify common pitfalls and vulnerabilities and take proactive measures to avoid falling victim to similar threats.

One common theme that emerges from many privacy violation cases is the failure to adequately assess and mitigate risks. In Sarah's case, for example, the lack of thorough background checks and security measures allowed the hidden camera to go undetected until it was too late. By implementing stricter guidelines for rental properties and conducting regular inspections, hosts can reduce the likelihood of covert surveillance and ensure the safety and privacy of their guests.

Similarly, Michael's experience underscores the importance of bystander intervention and community awareness in combating voyeurism and Peeping Tom's behavior. By speaking up and reporting suspicious activity, individuals can help deter would-be perpetrators and create a safer environment for everyone. Additionally, public education campaigns and awareness-raising initiatives can empower individuals to recognize the signs of voyeurism and take proactive steps to protect themselves and others from privacy violations.

However, real-life stories and case studies serve as powerful reminders of the pervasive threat posed by hidden cameras and Peeping Toms. By unveiling the realities of privacy violations and learning from the experiences of others, we can better understand the risks we face and take proactive measures to safeguard our privacy and security. Through vigilance, awareness, and community action, we can create a safer and more secure environment for ourselves and future generations.

CHAPTER 3

Mastering Awareness: How to Stay Vigilant in Any Setting

In a world where privacy violations lurk around every corner, mastering awareness is essential for staying vigilant and safeguarding your privacy in any setting. By developing a mindful mindset and honing your ability to identify potential camera locations, you can better protect yourself from the threat of hidden cameras and Peeping Toms.

Developing a Mindful Mindset: Being Aware of Your Surroundings

The first step in mastering awareness is cultivating a mindful mindset that allows you to stay present and attentive to your surroundings. Mindfulness involves intentionally paying attention to the present moment without judgment, allowing you to notice subtle details and cues that may indicate potential threats or hazards.

One effective way to cultivate mindfulness is through mindfulness meditation, a practice that involves focusing your attention on your breath, bodily sensations, or present-moment experiences. By incorporating mindfulness meditation into your daily routine, you can train your brain to become more attuned to your surroundings and better equipped to detect potential threats.

In addition to formal mindfulness practices, there are also everyday strategies you can use to enhance your awareness. For example, practicing active listening during conversations can help you stay engaged and alert to verbal cues that may indicate deception or dishonesty. Similarly, regularly checking in with yourself and tuning into your physical sensations can help you stay grounded and connected to the present moment.

By developing a mindful mindset and practicing mindfulness techniques regularly, you can sharpen your awareness and increase your ability to detect potential privacy violations in any setting.

Identifying Potential Camera Locations: Tips and Tricks

Once you've cultivated a mindful mindset, the next step is to become adept at identifying potential camera locations and recognizing the signs of covert surveillance. Hidden cameras can be concealed in a variety of everyday objects and locations, making them difficult to detect without careful observation.

One of the most important tips for identifying potential camera locations is to trust your instincts and pay attention to any feelings of discomfort or unease you may experience in a particular environment. If something feels off or out of place, take the time to investigate further and look for signs of hidden cameras or surveillance devices.

Another useful strategy is to familiarize yourself with common hiding spots and concealment techniques used by Peeping Toms and covert surveillance operators. For example, hidden cameras are often placed in strategic locations such as smoke detectors, alarm clocks, or electrical outlets, where they can capture video and audio footage without attracting attention.

To identify potential camera locations, be on the lookout for suspicious objects or anomalies that seem out of place in the environment. Pay attention to any unusual wires, lenses, or protrusions that may indicate the presence of a hidden camera. Additionally, keep an eye out for tiny flashing lights or indicators that may betray the presence of a surveillance device.

In some cases, you may need to employ additional tools and techniques to detect hidden cameras effectively. For example, using a flashlight to inspect mirrors or other reflective surfaces can help you spot hidden cameras that may be concealed behind them. Similarly, investing in a hidden camera detector or using a smartphone app designed to detect surveillance devices can provide an added layer of protection against privacy violations.

By mastering awareness and developing a mindful mindset, you can enhance your ability to stay vigilant and protect yourself from the threat of hidden cameras and Peeping Toms in any setting. By remaining present, attentive, and proactive, you can safeguard your privacy and security and enjoy greater peace of mind in your daily life.

CHAPTER 4

Tools of Defense: Hidden Camera Detection Techniques

In the ongoing battle against hidden cameras and the invasion of privacy they represent, arming oneself with the right tools of defense is crucial. Hidden camera detection techniques have evolved alongside the advancements in surveillance technology, offering individuals effective means to protect their privacy and security. In this section, we will explore the various tools available for detecting hidden cameras, including hidden camera detectors and detection apps, and how they can be used to your advantage.

Introduction to Hidden Camera Detectors

Hidden camera detectors are specialized devices designed to detect the presence of hidden cameras and other surveillance devices. These detectors utilize a variety of methods to identify potential threats, including radio frequency (RF) scanning, lens detection, and infrared (IR) detection.

RF detectors work by scanning the surrounding area for radio frequency signals emitted by wireless cameras and other electronic devices. When a hidden camera is detected, the RF detector alerts the user with an audible or visual signal, indicating the presence of a potential threat.

Lens detection technology, on the other hand, relies on the reflection of light to detect the presence of camera lenses. By shining a light source across the room and carefully inspecting reflective surfaces such as mirrors, windows, and camera lenses, users can identify hidden cameras that may be concealed in the environment.

Infrared detection is another common method used in hidden camera detectors, particularly for detecting night vision or infrared cameras. These detectors emit pulses of infrared light and analyze the reflections to identify hidden cameras that may be operating in low-light or infrared mode.

Hidden camera detectors come in a variety of forms, ranging from handheld devices to smartphone apps and portable scanners. Some detectors are designed for general-purpose use and can detect a wide range of surveillance devices, while others are specialized for specific types of cameras or detection methods.

Using Technology to Your Advantage: Hidden Camera Detection Apps

In addition to dedicated hidden camera detectors, technology has also given rise to a new generation of hidden camera detection apps that can be installed on smartphones and other mobile devices. These apps leverage the built-in sensors and capabilities of smartphones to detect hidden cameras and other surveillance devices, offering users a convenient and portable solution for privacy protection.

Hidden camera detection apps use a variety of detection methods, including RF scanning, lens detection, and infrared detection, to identify potential threats in the surrounding area. Some apps also offer additional features such as GPS tracking, signal strength analysis, and real-time alerts, providing users with comprehensive protection against hidden cameras and other surveillance devices.

One of the key advantages of hidden camera detection apps is their portability and ease of use. With just a few taps on your smartphone screen, you can quickly scan your surroundings for hidden cameras and take proactive measures to protect your privacy. Whether you're staying in a hotel room, visiting a friend's house, or shopping in a department store, hidden camera detection apps provide a convenient and effective way to stay vigilant and safeguard your security.

However, it's important to note that hidden camera detection apps may have limitations compared to dedicated detectors, particularly in terms of accuracy and sensitivity. While apps can provide valuable assistance in identifying potential threats, they should be used as part of a comprehensive approach to privacy protection that includes physical inspection and manual detection methods.

In conclusion, hidden camera detection techniques offer valuable tools for protecting your privacy and security in an increasingly surveilled world. Whether you opt for a dedicated hidden camera detector or a smartphone app, mastering the use of these tools can help you stay vigilant and proactive in identifying and mitigating the threat of hidden cameras and other surveillance devices. By harnessing the power of technology and leveraging the latest advancements in detection technology, you can take control of your privacy and enjoy greater peace of mind in your daily life.

CHAPTER 5

Home Sweet (Spy-Free) Home: Securing Your Living Space

Your home should be your sanctuary, a place where you can relax and unwind without fear of intrusion or surveillance. However, with the proliferation of hidden cameras and covert surveillance devices, ensuring that your living space remains spy-free requires proactive measures and vigilance. In this section, we will explore strategies for securing your home against hidden cameras, including tips for conducting home inspections and safeguarding against rental and Airbnb camera risks.

Checking Your Own Space: Tips for Home Inspections

Conducting regular home inspections is an essential first step in safeguarding your living space against hidden cameras and other surveillance devices. By familiarizing yourself with common hiding spots and concealment techniques, you can better identify potential threats and take proactive measures to protect your privacy and security.

Start by thoroughly inspecting each room in your home, paying close attention to areas where hidden cameras are most likely to be concealed. Common hiding spots include smoke detectors, alarm clocks, electrical outlets, and wall decorations, as well as less obvious locations such as air vents, ceiling tiles, and houseplants.

When conducting your inspection, be sure to check for any signs of tampering or unusual behavior, such as unexpected changes in device behavior, unexplained noises, or suspicious wires or cables. Additionally, consider investing in a hidden camera detector or using a smartphone app designed to detect surveillance devices, which can provide an added layer of protection against hidden threats.

In addition to physical inspections, it's also important to be mindful of your digital security and privacy. Regularly update your home Wi-Fi network password and enable encryption to prevent unauthorized access to your network. To further secure your internet connection and keep your online activity hidden from prying eyes, think about utilizing a virtual private network, or VPN.

By staying vigilant and proactive in conducting home inspections, you can reduce the risk of hidden cameras and other surveillance devices infiltrating your living space and enjoy greater peace of mind in your personal space.

Safeguarding Against Rental and Airbnb Camera Risks

The rise of short-term rental platforms such as Airbnb has made it easier than ever to book accommodations for travel or temporary stays. However, the convenience of these platforms also comes with inherent risks, including the possibility of encountering hidden cameras or other surveillance devices in rental properties.

To safeguard against rental and Airbnb camera risks, it's important to take proactive measures to protect your privacy and security when booking accommodations. Start by carefully reviewing the listing description and photos for any mention of security cameras or surveillance devices. Look for explicit disclosures about the presence of cameras and ask the host for clarification if necessary.

When you arrive at the rental property, conduct a thorough inspection of the premises to check for any hidden cameras or surveillance devices. Pay close attention to areas where cameras are most likely to be concealed, such as bedrooms, bathrooms, and common areas. Use a flashlight to inspect mirrors, decorative objects, and electronic devices for any signs of hidden cameras.

In addition to physical inspections, consider using a hidden camera detector or smartphone app to scan the rental property for surveillance devices. These tools can help you identify potential threats and take proactive measures to protect your privacy and security while staying in unfamiliar accommodations.

If you discover a hidden camera or surveillance device in your rental property, report it to the rental platform immediately and document your findings with photos or video evidence. Depending on the severity of the situation, you may choose to seek alternative accommodations or escalate the issue to local authorities.

By staying vigilant and proactive in safeguarding against rental and Airbnb camera risks, you can protect your privacy and security while enjoying the convenience and flexibility of short-term rentals. Remember to trust your instincts and prioritize your safety when booking accommodations, and don't hesitate to speak up if you have any concerns about hidden cameras or surveillance devices in your rental property.

CHAPTER 6

Beyond the Basics: Advanced Strategies for Privacy Protection

As technology continues to advance and privacy concerns become increasingly complex, it's important to go beyond the basics and explore advanced strategies for privacy protection. In this section, we will delve into two key aspects of privacy protection: maintaining privacy while traveling and understanding legal considerations and recourse options for privacy violations.

Maintaining Privacy While Traveling

Traveling can present unique challenges when it comes to privacy protection. Whether you're staying in a hotel, renting a vacation home, or simply exploring a new city, it's important to take proactive measures to safeguard your privacy and security while on the go.

One of the most effective ways to maintain privacy while traveling is to be mindful of your surroundings and take steps to minimize your exposure to potential threats. For example, avoid discussing sensitive or personal information in public places where you may be overheard, and be cautious when using public Wi-Fi networks to access sensitive data or conduct financial transactions.

When booking accommodations, carefully review the privacy policies and security measures of the hotel or rental property to ensure that your personal information will be protected. Consider opting for accommodations with secure access controls, such as keycard entry or digital locks, to reduce the risk of unauthorized access to your room.

Additionally, consider using a virtual private network (VPN) to encrypt your internet connection and protect your online activities from potential eavesdropping or surveillance. VPNs create a secure tunnel between your device and the internet, preventing third parties from intercepting your data and monitoring your online activities.

Finally, be vigilant about physical security risks while traveling, such as theft or unauthorized access to your belongings. Use a secure luggage lock to protect your belongings while in transit, and consider using a portable safe or security bag to store valuables such as passports, cash, and electronics while at your destination.

By staying mindful of your surroundings and taking proactive measures to protect your privacy and security while traveling, you can enjoy a worry-free travel experience and minimize the risk of privacy violations.

Legal Considerations and Recourse Options

In the event that your privacy is violated, it's important to understand your legal rights and recourse options for seeking justice and holding perpetrators accountable. Depending on the nature and severity of the privacy violation, you may have legal grounds for pursuing civil or criminal action against the responsible parties.

One of the most common legal remedies for privacy violations is the filing of a civil lawsuit seeking damages for invasion of privacy. Invasion of privacy encompasses a wide range of conduct, including eavesdropping, surveillance, and the unauthorized disclosure of private information. If you believe that your privacy has been violated, consult with a qualified attorney to discuss your legal options and determine the best course of action.

In addition to civil lawsuits, there may also be criminal penalties for certain types of privacy violations, such as voyeurism or unauthorized surveillance. Depending on the jurisdiction and the specific circumstances of the case, perpetrators of privacy violations may face criminal charges and potential imprisonment.

In cases where privacy violations involve the use of electronic surveillance or hacking, there may also be federal or state laws governing wiretapping, computer fraud, or other related offenses. Consult with a knowledgeable attorney who specializes in privacy law to understand the legal implications of your situation and explore potential avenues for legal recourse.

In addition to legal remedies, there are also non-legal options for addressing privacy violations, such as reporting the incident to law enforcement or regulatory authorities. Depending on the jurisdiction and the severity of the violation, law enforcement agencies may conduct investigations and pursue criminal charges against the responsible parties.

Ultimately, the most effective approach to addressing privacy violations is to take proactive measures to prevent them from occurring in the first place. By staying informed about privacy risks and implementing robust privacy protection measures, you can minimize the likelihood of falling victim to privacy violations and enjoy greater peace of mind in your daily life.

However, maintaining privacy while traveling and understanding legal considerations and recourse options are essential components of a comprehensive approach to privacy protection. By staying vigilant, informed, and proactive, you can safeguard your privacy and security in an increasingly interconnected and surveilled world.

CHAPTER 7

Empowering Yourself: Building a Personalized Privacy Plan

In today's digital age, where our personal information is constantly at risk of being compromised, empowering yourself with a personalized privacy plan is essential for safeguarding your most sensitive data and maintaining control over your digital footprint. By assessing your individual privacy needs and creating a customized privacy protection strategy, you can take proactive steps to protect yourself from privacy violations and preserve your online security.

Assessing Your Individual Privacy Needs

The first step in building a personalized privacy plan is to assess your individual privacy needs and identify areas of vulnerability. Start by conducting a thorough audit of your digital footprint, including your online accounts, social media profiles, and digital devices. Take note of the types of personal information you share online, such as your name, address, date of birth, and financial details, as well as any potential privacy risks associated with these disclosures.

Next, consider your online habits and behaviors, such as the websites you visit, the apps you use, and the information you share with others. Are you aware of the privacy policies and security measures of the platforms you use? Do you take precautions to protect your personal information, such as using strong, unique passwords and enabling two-factor authentication?

Finally, think about your offline privacy needs and concerns. Are you comfortable with the level of surveillance in your home or workplace? Do you take steps to protect your physical privacy, such as using window coverings or securing your mail?

By taking the time to assess your individual privacy needs and identify areas of vulnerability, you can gain valuable insights into the specific risks you face and develop a personalized privacy protection strategy tailored to your unique circumstances.

Creating a Customized Privacy Protection Strategy

Once you've assessed your individual privacy needs, the next step is to create a customized privacy protection strategy that addresses your specific concerns and vulnerabilities. This strategy should encompass a range of proactive measures designed to mitigate privacy risks and enhance your online security.

Start by implementing strong privacy settings on your devices and online accounts, such as enabling privacy-enhancing features like end-to-end encryption and disabling location tracking when not in use. Review the privacy policies of the platforms you use regularly and adjust your settings accordingly to minimize the amount of personal information you share with third parties.

Consider using privacy-enhancing tools and technologies to further protect your personal information online, such as virtual private networks (VPNs), ad blockers, and encrypted messaging apps. These tools can help you maintain anonymity and privacy while browsing the web and communicating with others online.

In addition to digital privacy measures, don't overlook the importance of physical security and privacy in your daily life. Take steps to secure your home and workplace against unauthorized access, such as installing security cameras, alarm systems, and door locks. Be vigilant about protecting your personal belongings and sensitive documents, both at home and while traveling.

Finally, stay informed about emerging privacy threats and best practices for privacy protection by regularly educating yourself about privacy-related issues and staying up-to-date on the latest developments in privacy law and technology. Consider joining online communities or forums dedicated to privacy advocacy and activism, where you can share information and resources with like-minded individuals.

By creating a customized privacy protection strategy that addresses your individual needs and concerns, you can take proactive steps to safeguard your personal information and maintain control over your digital footprint. By staying informed, vigilant, and proactive, you can empower yourself to navigate the complexities of the digital age with confidence and peace of mind.

CHAPTER 8

Community Awareness and Advocacy: Spreading Knowledge and Taking Action

In the fight against hidden camera threats and privacy violations, community awareness and advocacy play a crucial role in spreading knowledge and taking action to protect individual privacy rights. By educating others about hidden camera threats and supporting legislation and initiatives for privacy rights, communities can work together to create a safer and more secure environment for all.

Educating Others About Hidden Camera Threats

One of the most important aspects of community awareness and advocacy is educating others about the hidden camera threats that exist in our society. Many people are unaware of the prevalence of hidden cameras and how they can be used to violate privacy rights. By raising awareness about these threats, communities can empower individuals to take proactive steps to protect themselves and their loved ones.

Educational initiatives can take many forms, from public awareness campaigns and community workshops to online resources and educational materials. These initiatives can provide information about the different types of hidden cameras, common hiding spots, and signs of surveillance, as well as tips for detecting and preventing privacy violations.

Schools, community centers, and neighborhood associations can all play a role in educating their members about hidden camera threats and promoting best practices for privacy protection. By working together to raise awareness and share information, communities can empower individuals to take control of their privacy and security in the digital age.

Supporting Legislation and Initiatives for Privacy Rights

In addition to raising awareness, community advocacy efforts can also focus on supporting legislation and initiatives that protect privacy rights and hold perpetrators of privacy violations accountable. This may involve advocating for stronger privacy laws, supporting legislative initiatives that regulate the use of surveillance technology, and lobbying for increased transparency and oversight of government surveillance programs.

Community organizations, advocacy groups, and grassroots movements can all play a role in advocating for privacy rights at the local, state, and national levels. By mobilizing community members, organizing public demonstrations, and engaging with elected officials, communities can make their voices heard and influence policy decisions that affect privacy rights.

Supporting legislation and initiatives for privacy rights can also involve collaborating with other stakeholders, such as law enforcement agencies, technology companies, and civil liberties organizations. By fostering dialogue and collaboration among diverse stakeholders, communities can work towards common-sense solutions that balance the need for security with respect for individual privacy rights.

Community awareness and advocacy are essential components of the fight against hidden camera threats and privacy violations. By educating others about hidden camera threats and supporting legislation and initiatives for privacy rights, communities can empower individuals to protect themselves and advocate for positive change.

Through educational initiatives and public awareness campaigns, communities can raise awareness about hidden camera threats and promote best practices for privacy protection. By working together to share information and resources, communities can empower individuals to take control of their privacy and security in the digital age.

Similarly, by supporting legislation and initiatives for privacy rights, communities can advocate for stronger privacy protections and hold perpetrators of privacy violations accountable. By mobilizing community members, engaging with elected officials, and collaborating with other stakeholders, communities can work towards common-sense solutions that protect privacy rights while ensuring public safety.

However, community awareness and advocacy are powerful tools in the fight against hidden camera threats and privacy violations. By working together to educate others about hidden camera threats and support legislation and initiatives for privacy rights, communities can create a safer and more secure environment for all.

CHAPTER 9

Staying Safe in the Digital Age: Online Privacy and Security

In today's digital age, where our lives are increasingly lived online, staying safe requires a proactive approach to protecting our privacy and security. Understanding the risks of online surveillance and implementing digital privacy measures are essential steps in safeguarding our personal information and maintaining control over our digital footprint.

Understanding Online Surveillance Risks

Online surveillance poses a significant threat to our privacy and security, as our digital activities are constantly monitored and tracked by various entities. From government agencies and corporations to cybercriminals and malicious hackers, numerous actors are seeking to exploit our personal information for their gain.

One of the most pervasive forms of online surveillance is data collection by tech companies and social media platforms. These companies track our browsing habits, search history, location data, and other online activities to build detailed profiles about us for targeted advertising and other purposes. While some may argue that this data collection is necessary for providing personalized services, it also raises serious privacy concerns about the misuse of our personal information.

Government surveillance is another major threat to online privacy, with intelligence agencies around the world engaging in mass surveillance programs to monitor communications and gather intelligence. These programs often operate in secret, without adequate oversight or accountability, raising serious concerns about civil liberties and the erosion of privacy rights.

In addition to these threats, individuals also face risks from cybercriminals and malicious hackers who seek to exploit vulnerabilities in our digital devices and networks for financial gain or other malicious purposes. From phishing scams and malware attacks to identity theft and data breaches, the dangers of online surveillance are ever-present in our digital lives.

Implementing Digital Privacy Measures

To protect ourselves from the risks of online surveillance, it's important to implement digital privacy measures that can help mitigate these threats and enhance our online security. These measures encompass a range of proactive steps designed to safeguard our personal information and maintain control over our digital footprint.

One of the most fundamental digital privacy measures is to use strong, unique passwords for each of your online accounts and enable two-factor authentication whenever possible. This helps prevent unauthorized access to your accounts and reduces the risk of identity theft and account takeover.

Another important step is to review and adjust the privacy settings on your devices and online accounts to limit the amount of personal information you share with third parties. This may include adjusting your social media privacy settings, disabling location tracking on your smartphone, and opting out of targeted advertising networks.

Using privacy-enhancing tools and technologies can also help protect your online privacy and security. Virtual private networks (VPNs) encrypt your internet connection and mask your IP address, making it more difficult for third parties to track your online activities. Ad blockers and tracker blockers can prevent advertisers and data brokers from tracking your browsing habits and collecting your personal information.

In addition to these technical measures, it's also important to practice good digital hygiene and be cautious about the information you share online. Avoid clicking on suspicious links or downloading files from unknown sources, and be vigilant about phishing attempts and other common online scams.

By taking proactive steps to protect our online privacy and security, we can reduce the risks of online surveillance and maintain control over our digital lives. By understanding the threats we face and implementing digital privacy measures, we can stay safe in the digital age and enjoy greater peace of mind in our online interactions.

However, staying safe in the digital age requires a proactive approach to protecting our online privacy and security. By understanding the risks of online surveillance and implementing digital privacy measures, we can safeguard our personal information and maintain control over our digital footprint. By staying informed, vigilant, and proactive, we can navigate the complexities of the digital landscape with confidence and peace of mind.

CHAPTER 10

Future Trends and Emerging Technologies: Anticipating and Addressing New Threats

As technology continues to evolve at a rapid pace, so too do the threats to our privacy and security. To stay ahead of emerging risks and challenges, it's essential to explore future trends and anticipate how new technologies may impact our digital lives. By adapting our strategies to address evolving privacy concerns, we can better protect ourselves and safeguard our personal information in an increasingly connected world.

Exploring Future Risks and Challenges

The future landscape of privacy and security is shaped by a variety of factors, including advances in technology, changes in social norms, and shifts in regulatory frameworks. As we look ahead, several key trends and emerging technologies are likely to have a significant impact on our digital privacy and security.

One such trend is the proliferation of Internet of Things (IoT) devices, which are becoming increasingly integrated into our daily lives. From smart home devices and wearable technology to connected cars and smart cities, IoT devices collect vast amounts of data about our behaviors, preferences, and movements. While these devices offer convenience and efficiency, they also raise serious privacy concerns about the collection and use of personal data.

Another emerging technology with implications for privacy and security is artificial intelligence (AI) and machine learning. AI-powered algorithms are used in a wide range of applications, from predictive analytics and personalized recommendations to facial recognition and surveillance. While AI has the potential to improve efficiency and enhance decision-making, it also raises concerns about algorithmic bias, discrimination, and the erosion of privacy rights.

In addition to these trends, other emerging technologies such as quantum computing, biometrics, and blockchain also present both opportunities and challenges for privacy and security. Quantum computing has the potential to break traditional encryption algorithms, posing a threat to data security and privacy. Biometric technologies raise concerns about the collection and use of sensitive personal data, while blockchain introduces new possibilities for decentralized and secure data management.

Adapting Strategies to Stay Ahead of Evolving Privacy Concerns

To address these future risks and challenges, it's essential to adapt our strategies for protecting privacy and security to stay ahead of evolving threats. This requires a proactive approach that anticipates emerging risks and leverages new technologies to enhance our defenses.

One key strategy is to prioritize privacy and security by design, integrating privacy considerations into the design and development of new technologies and systems from the outset. By building privacy-enhancing features and security controls in IoT devices, AI algorithms, and other emerging technologies, we can reduce the risk of privacy violations and data breaches.

Another important strategy is to invest in research and development of privacy-preserving technologies and innovative security solutions. This may involve developing new encryption techniques, privacy-enhancing technologies, and decentralized data management systems that prioritize user control and data protection.

Education and awareness also play a crucial role in addressing emerging privacy concerns. By educating the public about the risks and implications of new technologies, we can empower individuals to make informed decisions about their digital privacy and security. This may involve providing resources and training on best practices for protecting personal information, as well as raising awareness about privacy rights and advocacy opportunities.

Collaboration and cooperation among stakeholders are also essential for addressing emerging privacy concerns effectively. This includes partnerships between government agencies, industry stakeholders, academia, and civil society organizations to develop policies, standards, and guidelines that promote privacy and security in the digital age.

By adapting our strategies to address evolving privacy concerns and leveraging new technologies to enhance our defenses, we can better protect ourselves and safeguard our personal information in an increasingly connected world. By staying informed, proactive, and collaborative, we can navigate the challenges of the future with confidence and resilience.

Appendix

Glossary of Terms

1. Hidden Camera: A surveillance camera that is concealed or disguised to monitor individuals without their knowledge or consent.

2. Privacy: The right to control access to one's personal information and the ability to maintain confidentiality and autonomy.

3. Surveillance: The monitoring, recording, and analysis of individuals' behavior, activities, or communications.

4. Data Breach: The unauthorized access, disclosure, or acquisition of sensitive information, such as personal or financial data.

5. Encryption: The process of encoding information to protect it from unauthorized access or interception.

6. Two-Factor Authentication (2FA): A security measure that requires users to provide two different forms of identification before granting access to an account or system.

7. Virtual Private Network (VPN): A secure network connection that allows users to access the internet privately and securely by encrypting their data and masking their IP address.

8. Phishing: A form of cyberattack in which attackers use deceptive emails, messages, or websites to trick individuals into revealing sensitive information, such as passwords or financial details.

9. Biometrics: The measurement and analysis of unique physical or behavioral characteristics, such as fingerprints or facial features, for identification and authentication purposes.

10. Blockchain: A decentralized digital ledger technology that records transactions across multiple computers in a way that is secure, transparent, and tamper-resistant.

Additional Resources and References

1. Electronic Frontier Foundation (EFF): https://www.eff.org/

2. Privacy International: https://privacyinternational.org/

3. National Cyber Security Centre (NCSC): https://www.ncsc.gov.uk/

4. Federal Trade Commission (FTC) - Consumer Information: https://www.consumer.ftc.gov/topics/privacy-security

5. Center for Democracy & Technology (CDT): https://cdt.org/

Frequently Asked Questions (FAQs) about Hidden Cameras and Privacy Protection

1. What are hidden cameras, and why are they a concern for privacy?

Hidden cameras are surveillance cameras that are concealed or disguised to monitor individuals without their knowledge or consent. They raise concerns for privacy because they can be used to invade individuals' privacy, violate their rights, and capture sensitive information without their consent.

2. Where are hidden cameras commonly found?

Hidden cameras can be found in a variety of settings, including public places such as stores, hotels, and restaurants, as well as private spaces such as homes, offices, and changing rooms. They may be concealed in everyday objects such as clocks, smoke detectors, and electrical outlets.

3. How can I detect hidden cameras?

There are several methods for detecting hidden cameras, including physical inspection, using a hidden camera detector device or app, and checking for suspicious behavior or signs of surveillance. It's important to be vigilant and take precautions to protect your privacy in both public and private settings.

4. What steps can I take to protect my privacy from hidden cameras?

To protect your privacy from hidden cameras, consider taking precautions such as being mindful of your surroundings, checking for signs of surveillance, and using privacy-enhancing tools and technologies such as VPNs and encryption. It's also important to advocate for stronger privacy protections and support initiatives that promote privacy rights.

5. What should I do if I suspect that I'm being monitored by a hidden camera?

If you suspect that you're being monitored by a hidden camera, it's important to take immediate action to protect your privacy and security. This may involve leaving the area, reporting your concerns to the appropriate authorities, and seeking legal advice if necessary.

These FAQs provide basic information about hidden cameras and privacy protection. For more detailed information and guidance, consult additional resources and consider seeking advice from privacy experts and legal professionals.

CONCLUSION

In today's interconnected world, where digital technologies are deeply integrated into every aspect of our lives, safeguarding our privacy and security has never been more important. From hidden cameras in public spaces to data breaches and online surveillance, the threats to our privacy are ever-present and evolving.

Throughout this book, we've explored the various ways in which our privacy can be compromised and the strategies we can employ to protect ourselves. We've learned about the different types of hidden cameras and how to detect them, as well as the importance of staying vigilant and proactive in safeguarding our personal information.

We've also delved into the world of online privacy and security, examining the risks of data collection and surveillance by tech companies, governments, and cybercriminals. We've explored the role of emerging technologies such as artificial intelligence and blockchain in shaping the future of privacy and security, and we've discussed the importance of adapting our strategies to address evolving threats.

But perhaps most importantly, we've emphasized the power of education, awareness, and advocacy in protecting our privacy rights. By staying informed about the risks we face and the tools and techniques available to mitigate them, we can empower ourselves to take control of our digital lives and protect our personal information.

As we move forward, we must remain vigilant and proactive in defending our privacy and security. We must continue to advocate for stronger privacy protections, support initiatives that promote transparency and accountability, and work together to create a safer and more secure online environment for all.

Ultimately, safeguarding our privacy is not just about protecting our personal information—it's about preserving our autonomy, dignity, and fundamental rights as individuals. By taking action to protect our privacy today, we can help shape a future where privacy is respected and valued by all.

www.ingramcontent.com/pod-product-compliance
Lightning Source LLC
Chambersburg PA
CBHW070925220526
45470CB00014B/1915